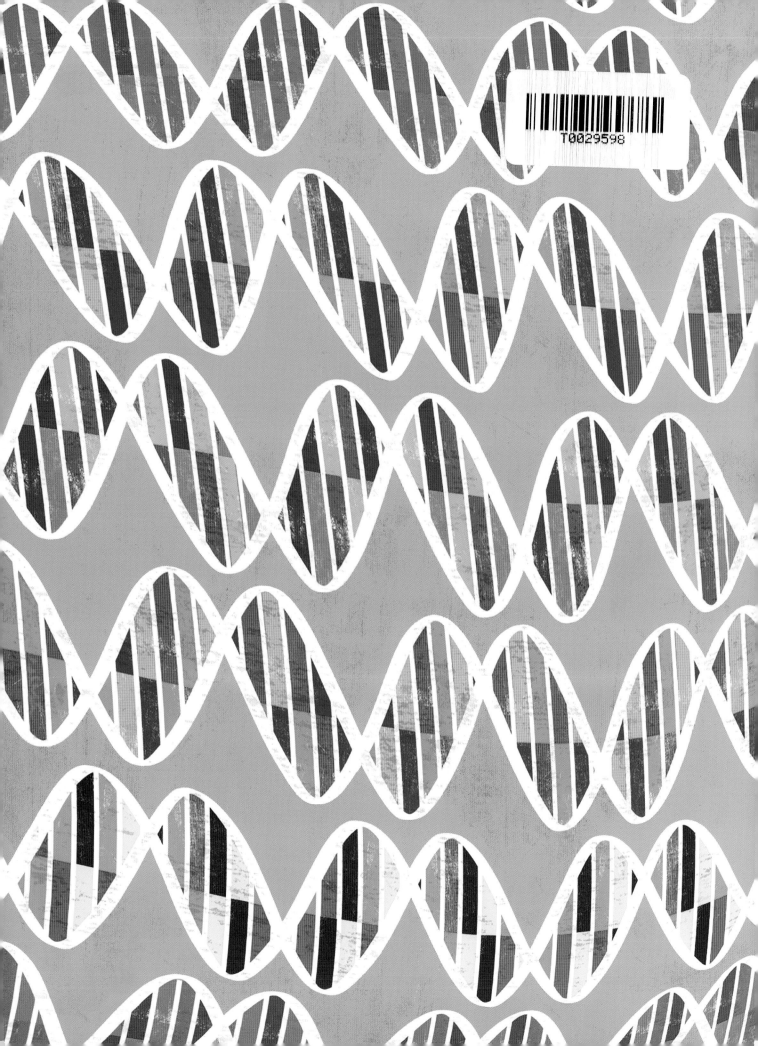

For Ann Bramlage Heerens, an incredible
classmate, doctor, and friend
—RL

To my sister Debra, whose
DNA is a force of love and care
—SS

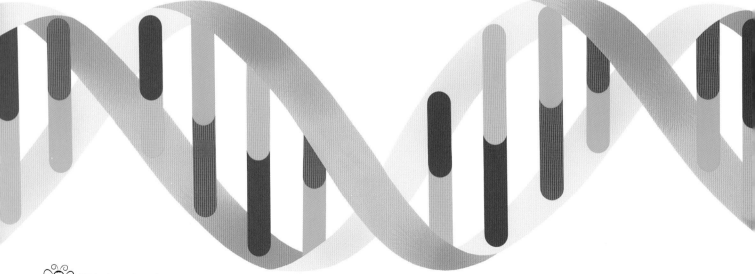

little bee books

New York, NY

Text copyright © 2021 by Rajani LaRocca | Illustrations copyright © 2021 by Steven Salerno | All rights reserved, including the right of reproduction in whole or in part in any form. | For information about special discounts on bulk purchases, please contact Little Bee Books at sales@littlebeebooks.com. | Manufactured in China RRD 0521
First Edition 10 9 8 7 6 5 4 3 2 1
ISBN 978-1-4998-1075-2 | littlebeebooks.com

the Secret CODE INSIDE YOU

all about your DNA

Rajani LaRocca, MD   illustrated by Steven Salerno

little bee books

Why aren't you fuzzy like a dog,
or buzzy like a bee?

Why can't you eat ants with your nose,

or breathe beneath the sea?

Why aren't you finny like a fish,
or grinny like a shark?

Why can't you catch flies with your tongue,

or
see
things
in
the
dark?

Why aren't you leapy like a frog,
or creepy like a spider?

Why can't you sit and lay an egg,

or be
your own
hang glider?

Now when you think of life that grows
with leaves or fur or wings,
cells are the tiny building blocks
of all earth's living things.

How To Be A Bear

And in the center of each cell,
too small for eyes to see,
there lie detailed instructions
for what it's supposed to be.

There's a secret code inside you,
a code called *DNA*.
A code that tells your body's cells
what they should do each day.

It looks like twisted ladders,
or tiny, twirling noodles.
It makes us into people,

DNA

instead of into poodles.

A lamb grows up to be a sheep,
and not a kangaroo.

A chick becomes a chicken,

and you grow into YOU.

You notice in the mirror
that you have your father's nose.
You might look at your wiggly feet
and see your mother's toes.

You wonder every single day
if you'll be short or tall.
And will your ears be giant-sized;
your hands be large or small?

The secret code inside you
is split up into *genes*.

Unraveled and decoded,

they're used to make proteins.

The proteins from your DNA
make muscles, bones, and skin.
They dictate what you look like

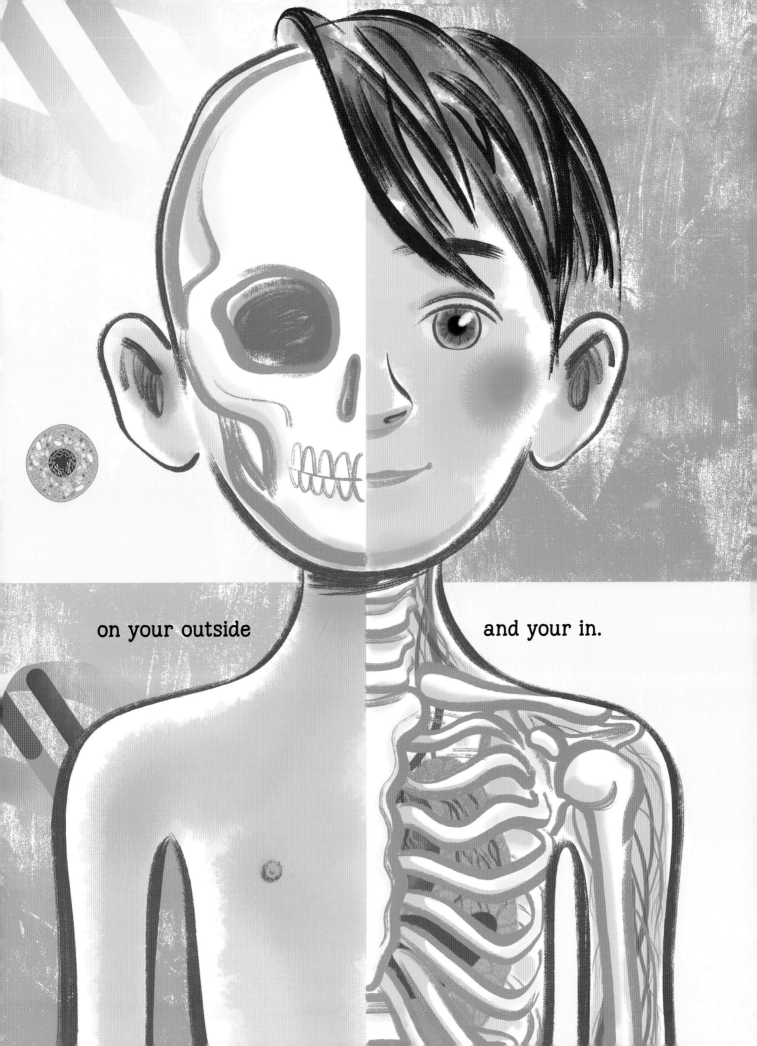

on your outside

and your in.

Each biological parent
gave you half your *chromosomes*.
And on those special forty-six,
your genes all make their homes.

Your code came from those parents,
and from their parents, too.
You might share genes with those you love
or some you never knew.

It's coiled inside of every cell,
those tiny, twisted ladders.
Your code makes you uniquely you,
but it's not all that matters.

It makes the color of your eyes,
but YOU choose where to look:
at butterflies or sunset skies,
or even at this book.

It gives you muscles small or large,
but YOU choose how to move.

You skip,

or jump,

or flip,

or roll.

You dance to your own groove.

The code gives you amazing hands,
but YOU choose how to play:

with trucks,

or balls,

or blocks,

or clay.

or paints,

with drums,

or dolls,

The code gives you an awesome brain,
but YOU choose what you'll be:
a teacher, doctor, or explorer
of space, sky, or sea!

The secret code inside you
is how you are designed.
The actions you choose every day
make YOU one of a kind!

DNA Facts

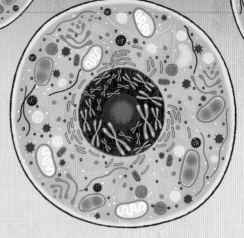

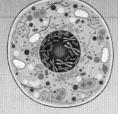

◊ Every living thing is made up of smaller parts called **cells**. Cells are so small that in most cases, you can't see them with your eyes or even with a magnifying glass; you may need a special scientific instrument called a **microscope**.

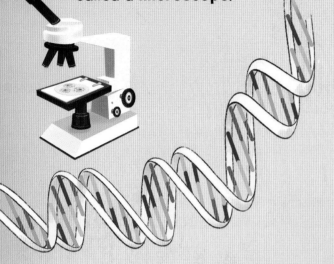

◊ Your body has about 30 trillion cells! Inside the center (nucleus) of every cell in your body is a secret code called **DNA**, which is short for **D**eoxyribo**N**ucleic **A**cid.

◊ DNA was discovered by scientists in 1869, but they didn't know what it looked like until 1953. It looks like two little strands coiled in a twisted ladder shape called a **double helix**.

◊ DNA is coiled and compressed into structures called **chromosomes**. Humans have 23 pairs of chromosomes in each and every cell—46 in total. You get half your DNA (23 chromosomes) from your biological mother, and half (23 chromosomes) from your biological father. This refers to "mother," "father," and "parent" in terms of their biological definitions. There are all kinds of families, and you may not share genes with those who raise you, but you are family just the same.

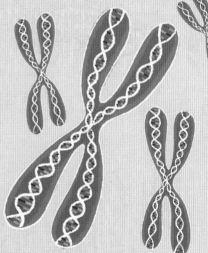

◊ Siblings get their DNA from the same parents, but unless they're identical twins, the combination of the DNA is different for each person.

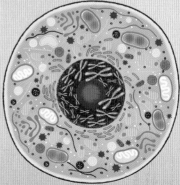

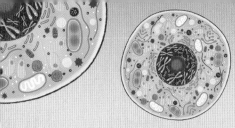

◊ On each chromosome, DNA is grouped into units called **genes**. Your genes are the blueprint for how you look, including your hair and eye color, your height, and whether you have dimples. They also determine all kinds of things you can't see, like your blood type and even whether you might be more likely to get certain diseases.

◊ A gene is **decoded** using **transcription**, in which a temporary copy is made of the gene, and then the cell uses that copy in a process called **translation** to make a protein. Each gene is a code for a protein that affects how your cells work—which makes skin cells different from bone cells or heart cells, and also makes your cells different from animal cells, plant cells, and the cells of any other person.

◊ If you unraveled and laid out all of a single cell's DNA end to end, it would be about 6 feet long.

◊ If you placed all of the DNA in your body end to end, it would stretch to the sun and back over 120 times!

◊ Every person shares 99.9% of their DNA with all other people.

◊ We have about 96-98% of our DNA in common with chimpanzees.

◊ We have about 50% of our DNA in common with bananas!

And you can learn more about DNA at these websites:

- history.nih.gov/exhibits/genetics/kids.htm
- easyscienceforkids.com/dna-your-bodys-blueprints/
- amnh.org/explore/ology/genetics#all

Banana DNA Experiment

You'll need a grown-up's help to do this experiment to see the DNA in a banana.

Materials

◊ ½ ripe banana, peeled

◊ ½ cup hot water

◊ 1 tsp salt

◊ ½ tsp liquid dishwashing soap

◊ quart-sized resealable zip-top plastic bag

◊ bottle of 90-100% rubbing (isopropyl) alcohol, put in freezer at least two hours ahead of time or overnight

◊ coffee filter

◊ narrow-mouthed glass that can hold at least 1 cup of liquid

◊ tape

◊ wooden stirrer

Procedure

1. Put the banana in the plastic bag, and mash it gently until all the lumps are gone and it resembles a mushy pudding.

2. Mix the salt and the hot water. Carefully pour this into the bag with the banana. Seal the bag, and mash the salt water and banana gently through the bag for about a minute.

3. Add the dishwashing soap and mix very gently. Avoid making too much foam.

4. Put the coffee filter on top of the glass, taping the top in place so it doesn't move.

5. Pour the banana mash into the filter, allowing the liquid to drip down into the glass. Once all the liquid has drained, remove and throw away the filter and its solid contents.

6. Take the rubbing alcohol out of the freezer. Tilt the glass and slowly pour the alcohol down the inside of the glass so the two liquids don't mix and the rubbing alcohol forms a layer about 1-2 inches deep on top of the banana liquid.

7. Wait for eight to ten minutes. You may see bubbles or clumps forming in the layer of rubbing alcohol.

8. Taking the stirrer, poke at the clumps in the alcohol layer and twirl to gather some up. Remove the stirrer and look at the clumps. This is banana DNA! With just your eyes, you can see lots of DNA clumped together, but you'll need a special microscope to see the double helix shape of individual strands of DNA.

In this experiment, we mashed banana with salt water and dish soap, then poured a layer of rubbing alcohol on top. All of these steps helped extract the banana DNA because:

- The mashing helps physically break down cell walls.

- Dish soap breaks down the lipid (fat) layers of cell membranes and nuclei, releasing the DNA from the nuclei.

- DNA can dissolve in some liquids, but not in alcohol, so when the DNA gets to the alcohol layer, it starts forming clumps.

- Salt helps the DNA stick together in clumps large enough for us to see.

- Since DNA is in every living thing, you can do this experiment with any fruit or vegetable.

Selected Bibliography

Miko, I. & LeJeune, L., eds. *Essentials of Genetics*. Cambridge, MA: NPG Education, 2009.
Last updated: January 17, 2014. nature.com/scitable/ebooks/essentials-of-genetics-8/126042179

Newman, Tim. "What is DNA and how does it work?" *Medical News Today*, updated January 11, 2018.
medicalnewstoday.com/articles/319818.php